Coinage of the United States – A Short History

Doug West, Ph.D.

Table of Contents

Preface

Welcome to the book *Coinage of the United States – A Short History*. This book is part of the *30 Minute Book Series* and, as the name of the series implies, if you are an average reader this book will take around 30 minutes to read. Since this book is not meant to be an all-encompassing story of United States coinage, you may want to know more about this interesting subject. To help you with this, there are several good references at the end of this book. To assist you with terms you may not be familiar with, a glossary is included. Thank you for purchasing this book and I hope you enjoy your time reading about the history of United States coinage.

Doug West

October 2015

Introduction

The story of United States coinage is really just a reflection of the history of America. The young nation just being formed struggled to supply a steady stream of coinage to the citizens so they could go about their day-to-day lives, buying and selling their products, and purchasing the items they needed for their lives. Up until the end of the Civil War, the coins the typical American found in their pocket or purse could have as easily been from France, England, Spain, or the United States. Maybe at their local merchant they would pay with some paper money issued by the bank down the street, and receive as change some privately issued merchant tokens that were good for trade again with that storekeeper. For the first century of American life, having plenty of small change in your pocket to complete a transaction was a real luxury.

The founding fathers set the stage for a coinage system. They didn't even mention paper money; instead, they based the system upon the sound financial basis of gold and silver. Over the centuries, however, this was a constant headache for the Treasury Department as the values of the precious metals were always changing. By the turn of the twentieth century, coin shortages were rare and the designs of the coins started taking on a much more artistic flare. President Theodore Roosevelt was instrumental in the change from a formal standard design to a more symbolic and artistic coinage. Some of the finest sculptors in the country would compete to have their design adopted for a new coin series. It would be in 1933 that America effectively abandoned the gold standard and based the coinage on the good faith of the government and silver coins. By 1964, even the silver had been removed from the coinage, being replaced with base metals, such as copper, nickel, and zinc.

Read on and learn about the history of the money in our pockets.

CHAPTER 1

Coins in Colonial America

When the explorers came from Europe to start exploring and conquering the new world, what we now call North and South America, they were primarily looking for wealth in the form of precious metals. After traipsing around the Eastern part of North America for a few decades, they came to the realization that this part of the new world was metal poor. They had better luck in Central and South America with silver depositions. The Spanish quickly set up mining operations in Mexico and parts of South America and started producing the Spanish Eight reales coin.

The Spanish Eight reales coin or milled dollar, also called the *Pillar dollar* or *pieces of eight*, has a special place in the history of coinage. This was one of the most popular coins used in the early American colonies. The coin could be cut into fragments to become one, two, and four reales coins, hence the term "pieces of eight." One real had a value of 12-1/2 cents and was known as a *bit*. The eight reales coin would become the forerunner of the United States dollar and the fractional coins as we know them today. In 1776, Thomas Jefferson recommended to the Continental Congress that the silver Spanish milled dollar become the monetary unit of the new country. The eight reales coin has been struck by a variety of mints in different countries: Mexico, Bolivia, Chile, Colombia, Guatemala, and Peru.

Figure – 1776 Spanish Eight Reales Coin

The story of money in America starts in 1620 as the early European settlers in New England started trading with Native Americans for goods that could be exported to Britain and the European continent. The export of tobacco, lumber, and furs were used by the colonists to purchase much needed items that they could not produce locally. Trade was also carried out with the local Indians through the use of barter and strings of wampum. Wampum was made from shells of various colors, ground to the size of kernels of corn with a hole drilled through each piece so it could be strung on a leather thong and worn as jewelry if desired. Wampum was used as a medium of exchange up until the 1690s; by then, it had been deeply devalued by overproduction and adulteration. Beaver skins, wampum, and tobacco became a local medium of exchange for items the settlers needed from the Indians. Coins were of little value when dealing with the Indians; their use was with the traders that came from Europe to supply the colonists. They normally demanded payment for their goods in silver or gold coins.

In trade with Europe, nearly all foreign coins were accepted as trade for goods. The most popular coins were the French louis, English quines, German thalers, and various Spanish and Dutch coins. Due to their popularity, the pieces of eight were commonly used for trade. The Spanish milled dollar continued to remain the standard coinage through the colonial period and even after the United States Mint was established in 1792. The Spanish milled dollar circulated legally and widely through the country up until 1857.

The American colonists were chronically ignored by the English Crown and there was a shortage of hard currency for daily trade. The English trade system was built on exports from the colonies, and they sought to control trade by limiting the amount of "hard" money paid to the colonists. Under this system, the colonists were limited in their trade to England, primarily.

To solve the problem of a shortage of coinage to use in trade, the colonists started using a wide assortment of foreign coins and tokens in daily use. The first coins minted in America were made by John Hull and his partner, Robert Sanderson, in Boston, for the Massachusetts Bay Colony. He was given this authority by the General Court of the colony despite possible objections from the king of England. In 1652, the Massachusetts minter began producing silver shilling coins and fractional shillings; they were known as Willow, Oak, and Pine Tree shillings. The size of the coin varied with the denomination, and the design was simple, with the date, denomination, the words MASATHVSETS and NEW ENGLAND around the perimeter, and a picture of a different type of tree. A crude design was also produced with "NE," and a value in Roman numerals was on the coin. This run of the early coinage lasted from 1652 until 1682. The Massachusetts silver coins were the first silver coins made within the continental United States and they also saw circulation in Canada.

With one exception, these coins all date 1652. This was not a coincidence — the coins were dated 1652 to evade British law and because this was the first year they were minted. Under the law, the king had the sole right to produce coinage; however, there was no king in 1652, as Charles' head had been severed three years earlier. The colonists took advantage and kept minting the coins with the date of 1652.

The colonists were subjected to all types of private tokens and foreign coins in their day-to-day commerce. Lord Baltimore was responsible for an issue of silver coins that was sent to Maryland in 1659. Another coin in circulation at the time came from William Wood in England, and it was known as *Rosa Americana* and dated 1722 to 1724. In addition to coins produced in England, enterprising Americans created their own copper and brass pieces that circulated for decades within the colonies. In Annapolis, Maryland, John Chalmers, a silversmith, issued silver shillings, sixpence, and three pence pieces in 1783. A variety of English tokens and coins continued to arrive at the shores of North America. Small denomination copper coins were much needed to handle small transactions. As silver coins arrived in the colonies, they were routinely sent back to England for payment of taxes and merchandise needed by the colonists. The forms of money most commonly used in the colonies were copper coins and paper money issued by the individual states.

The American Revolutionary War officially came to an end in 1783 and the new country was deeply in debt to finance the war effort. After the war, during the period 1781 to 1795, more English and American made tokens were made for the new country. The colonists had won the Revolutionary War but it exacted a large cost on the public — including shortage of currency, high taxes, and foreclosures from bankruptcies.

The Articles of Confederation, adopted March 1, 1781, granted Congress the sole right to regulate the alloy and value of coins by its own authority or by that of the respective states. This gave each state the right to coin their own money, with oversight from the Federal government. New Hampshire was the first state to take advantage of this new authority and minted a limited quantity of copper coins, all dating 1776.

During the period from 1785 to 1788, Connecticut, Vermont, and New Jersey granted the privilege to coin money to companies and individuals. During this period, the states produced a variety of coins that are found in today's coin collections. Boston was the home of the Mint for the state of Massachusetts and it produced copper coins from 1787 until 1788.

CHAPTER 2

United States Coinage – Early Attempts

Up until the signing of the Declaration of Independence in 1776, the colonists had been forced to deal with a wide array of foreign tokens and coinage, which made conversions rather cumbersome for transactions. It was a natural thing for the newly formed country to want its own coinage to facilitate trade domestically and with other countries. Shopkeepers had become accustomed to the Spanish dollar and its fractional parts, and it was a logical choice that this new national currency should be similar to this established coinage.

It was the norm in business at that time to quote contracts, currency statues, and prices in the colonies in terms of the Spanish dollar or in British pounds. The first issue of Continental paper money occurred on May 10, 1775, and it provided that the notes would be payable in "Spanish Milled Dollars or the value thereof in gold or silver."

The first attempt at producing a dollar coin as Continental currency came in 1776. The coin was struck in brass, pewter, and silver. Only a very limited number of silver pieces were struck. The pewter pieces were most likely intended as substitute for the paper dollars.

The new sovereign nation needed its own coinage system and one was proposed by the assistant financier of the Confederation, Gouverneur Morris, who proposed a coinage system designed to make conversion of various foreign currencies easier to convert to a dollar-sized unit. The plan was presented to Congress in January of 1782. Morris's plan was rather ingenious, but not very practical, with the fundamental unit of the system being 1/1,440 of a dollar. This system would allow conversion without a fraction to all the different valuation of the Spanish milled dollar used in the states.

Although a Mint for the new government was approved on February 21, 1782, it would be several years before coinage would be produced by the Mint. During 1784, Thomas Jefferson, who was then a member of the House of Representatives, expressed his concerns about Morris's complicated money unit and proposed a simpler system based on the dollar. He favored a dollar-based system because people were already familiar with the dollar as a unit of measure. In 1785, the Grand Committee recommended a gold five-dollar piece and a dollar of silver, with fraction coins of the same metal with denominations of a half, quarter, 1/10, and 1/20. The recommendation also called for fractional copper coinage valued at 1/100 and 1/200 of a dollar.

In 1783, the Superintendent of Finance, Robert Morris, submitted a series of silver pattern designs in decimal denominations that were known as the *Nova Constellatio* patterns. The coins consisted of a "mark" or 1,000 units; the "quint" or 500 units; and the "bit" or 100 units; and cover "five." These pattern pieces represent the first attempt at a decimal ratio, and were the forerunners of our present money units. The state of Massachusetts was the first to issue a cent and half-cent which were struck in 1787 and 1788. These were the first coins to be based on 1/100 and 1/200 parts of the Spanish dollar.

In May of 1787, 56 delegates from the individual states met in Philadelphia to discuss ways to improve the Articles of Confederation. The existing document was weak and the bulk of the power of governance lay with the individual states. Proponents of scrapping the Articles of Confederation and starting over with a new document were Alexander Hamilton and James Madison. The delegates, after much debate, came up with the United States Constitution of 1787. This new document gave the central government the power to put down uprisings, appoint Federal judges for life, set a four-year term on the office of the President, and many other changes were put forth in this historic document.

Section 8 of the Constitution gave the Federal government the power: "To coin Money, regulate the Value thereof, and of foreign Coin, and fix the Standard of Weights and Measures..." This clearly gave the government the power to coin money, but it does not state that the new government could print and circulate paper money. Hamilton and the fellow framers of the Constitution were deliberately vague here, as they intended the nation's monetary system to be built on "hard money"; that is, gold and silver coinage.

Section 10 referred to the form of money: "No state shall enter into a Treaty, alliance, or Confederation; grant Letters of Marque and Reprisal; coin Money; emit Bills of Credit; make anything but gold and silver Coin a Tender in Payment of Debts..." This purposefully took the authority to coin money away from the states and established gold and silver coin as the only medium for payments of debts. The new Constitution was completed in September, 1787, after more than a years' worth of debate and discussion. It would be 1790 before all the states had ratified the Constitution.

The first federally authorized coin was the Fugio copper. The obverse of the coin had a central design of a sundial surrounded by the legend, "1787 Fugio Mind Your Business," and the reverse had the legend, "United States We Are One," surrounded by thirteen interlacing rings, which represented the thirteen states. The Fugio copper is sometimes called the Franklin cent since it is believed that Benjamin Franklin supplied the design and legends. Fewer than 400,000 pieces were struck and they didn't see wide circulation.

Figure – 1787 Fugio Cent

The Secretary of the Treasury, Alexander Hamilton, reported his views on monetary matters on January 21, 1791, where he concurred with the decimal subdivisions and multiples of the dollar contained in earlier resolutions. Hamilton also advocated the use of both gold and silver in standard money of the United States.

CHAPTER 3

The United States Mint is Established

Congress passed a resolution on March 3, 1791, that a Mint be established, and authorizing President Washington to engage artists and procure machinery for the production of coins. On April 2, 1792, the Mint Act was passed, proving "that the money of account of the United States should be expressed in dollars or units, dismes or tenths, cents or hundredths, and milles or thousandths; a disme being the tenth part of a dollar, a cent the hundredth part of a dollar, a mille the thousandth part of a dollar..." The largest denomination authorized was the $10 gold eagle, which was to weight 270 grains. The standard purity for gold was to be an 11/12 fine gold alloy. The silver dollar was to weigh 416 grains, and the smallest denomination coin was the copper half-cent, which was specified to a weigh of 132 grains of pure copper. The silver coins were specified to be an 89.24 parts fine alloy. Both the gold and silver coins were alloyed with copper to improve their wear characteristic. Pure gold and silver are very soft metals and coins made from the pure metals would wear very quickly once in general circulation.

The well known scientist, David Rittenhouse, was appointed by President Washington as the first director of the Mint. Construction of a Mint building began in 1792, located on Seventh Street in Philadelphia. The first coin struck by the government was the half disme. Only fifteen hundred of these pieces were produced during the month of July 1792, which was before the Mint was complete. George Washington provided some of the silver, around $100 worth, needed for the new coin. The name disme was later changed to the name we are familiar with today, the dime.

Figure – George Washington, Alexander Hamilton, and Thomas Jefferson inspect the first coins. Seated is Martha Washington. Painting, *Inspecting the First Coins,* by John Dunsmore.

Silver and gold for coinage were to be supplied by the public. Under provision of the 1792 bill, the general public could have their gold and silver converted to coinage for only a one half of one percent fee. The copper for the new half-cents and cents was to be provided by the government. Congress had authorized the purchase of not more than 150 tons of copper. Six pounds of copper were purchased locally to begin preparation of coins, but thereafter, the copper was provided in the form of blank coins or planchets and was purchased from Boulton and Watt of Birmingham, England, from 1798 to 1838.

In 1792, before regular Mint operations began, several *patterns* or trial pieces were produced. Pattern coins are intended to demonstrate the size, form, and design of the proposed coins. One such pattern coin tested was a copper penny with a silver plug in the center. The silver was added to bring the intrinsic value of the coin up to the value of a penny. This pattern may have been generated from a comment made by Alexander Hamilton, that a penny made of pure copper would be too large and the silver would allow for a smaller sized coin. Until the Mint became fully operational, additional trial patterns were experimented with.

By 1794, the Mint had become operational with limited capability. The Bank of Maryland deposited the first silver in 1794. The first gold coined by the Mint was from Moses Brown, a Boston merchant, who deposited over two thousand dollars in the form of gold ingots in 1795.

By 1793, the Mint had limited production capability and was able to produce 111,512 cents and 35,334 half-cents. This was hardly enough to alleviate the chronic shortage of small coins required for commerce, but it was a good start. The first return of silver coins came in the fall of 1794, and the first gold coins were delivered in the summer of 1795. To maintain accurate weights and dimensions on the coins, the workers at the Mint would take the blank planchets and check for over or underweight planchets; overweight blanks were filed down to proper weight and underweight blanks were discarded. It is not uncommon to see evidence of this filing or adjustments made to coin blanks in the final coins that entered circulation. Coins from that era that were minted with crude equipment and essentially by hand, and they have many subtle differences that you won't see on today's mass produced coinage.

During the period 1793 to 1799, the Mint produced approximately $50,000 in cents and half-cents. This amount was insufficient to meet the needs of commerce, and as a result, foreign coins of various weights and purity continued to circulate within the nation for decades. Up until just before the Civil War, the Mint did not produce enough coinage to meet the demands of the growing nation. One of the problems that limited the circulation of gold and silver coins was the effect speculators had on the amount of coins in circulation. Worn and underweight Spanish dollars were exchanged for the freshly minted US silver dollars, which were then promptly exported, thus reducing the amount of coins in circulation. As part of the original specifications of United States coinage, the ratio of silver to gold was 15 to 1. When Alexander Hamilton proposed this ratio, it was in line with what was currently traded throughout the world. By 1799, the value ratio had shifted to 15-3/4 to 1. At this ratio, the gold coins were either melted for bullion or were shipped out of the country. As a result of this imbalance in the ratio of gold to silver, gold coins were rarely seen in circulation. To remedy this problem, President Jefferson suspended the coinage of silver and gold coins in 1804.

With the halt in production of gold and silver dollars, the largest denomination became the half dollar coin. For the first half of the nineteenth century, the half dollar circulated little and was used primarily for bank to bank transactions. The Mint did produce small quantities of quarters, dimes, and half dimes from 1794 to 1834; however, the quantities produced were small by today's standards. In 1830, it was estimated that the amount of coinage in circulation was only sufficient so that each person could only have one coin. The first three decades of the 1800s was a chaotic time for coins and currency. The Mint was not producing sufficient coinage to meet the demand of the public, so this forced the use of privately issued bank notes, foreign gold and silver coins, and privately issued tokens. Up until the national paper money commenced in 1861, private banks and institutions flooded the monetary systems with notes of questionable quality. When it came time to redeem your bank notes for gold or silver, the note might be worthless or redeemed at a deep discount to its face value.

The Mint and the coinage laws were completely revised in 1837. The new law required the standardization of gold and silver coins to 900 thousandths fineness. The gold ten-dollar eagle resumed production and silver dollars were produced in larger quantities.

By the 1820s, the Second Bank of the United States had a large influence over the nation's currency, but this all changed in 1832 when President Andrew Jackson vetoed a bill re-chartering the bank. This action caused instabilities in the economy and eventually led to a national financial crisis. Within five years of Jackson's veto, the country was so short on circulating currency that merchants began producing their own penny-sized tokens for commerce. The few available government issued coins were hoarded or converted, at a premium, to private, bank-issued paper money.

CHAPTER 4

The Rush for Gold

The first significant gold discovery in the United States came in North Carolina in 1799. This was a small discovery in comparison to the later finds, but it did contribute to the gold supply necessary to Mint coins. In 1835, a branch Mint was established in Charlotte, North Carolina, to mint the local gold into coins. The Mint's existence was short-lived due to the outbreak of the Civil War as the Confederacy took control of the Mint. The Confederate States of America continued minting gold coins at Charlotte until October 1861. It was then converted to a hospital for the remainder of the war.

In 1828, gold was discovered in Georgia and within a year the rush for Georgia gold was underway. Over the next few years, miners would flow into the state and boom towns like Auraria and Dahlonega sprang up. Much of the gold was on land held by the Cherokee Indians and this caused much tension between the miners and the Indians. Consistent with the times, President Andrew Jackson authorized the Indian Removal Act in 1830, which, among other things, allowed a takeover of the gold mining areas in Georgia.

In 1838, a branch Mint was established in Dahlonega, Georgia, to handle the gold mined in the region. The Mint produced gold coins up until 1861, in denominations of one dollar, two and one half dollars or quarter eagles, three dollar coins in 1854, and five dollar coins or half eagles. The Dahlonega Mint suffered a similar fate to the Charlotte Mint as it was taken over by the Confederate States of America and shut down in 1861.

Due to the short lifespans of the Charlotte and Dahlonega Mints, any surviving gold coins from these Mints are highly sought after by collectors today.

Figure – Reverse of the 1843-D Dahlonega Mint Half Eagle

With the discovery of gold in California in 1848, the push westward was on, and within a decade tens of thousands of people would flood into California seeking their fortune in gold. The state of California saw rapid growth because of the gold discovery, and the population of the state had grown from around 14,000 non-Indians before the discovery to nearly 250,000 by 1852. This mass migration to the West coast caused a severe shortage of coinage to meet the swelling demands of commerce. To solve this problem, enterprising individuals started minting their own gold coins. They came in all shapes and sizes, from the tiny 25-cent fractional gold coins to a hefty fifty dollar slug of gold. These new privately minted coins helped solve the shortage of coins and facilitated economic growth in the region. In 1854, the San Francisco Mint was opened and began coining money. It would take years until the new Mint had enough production to solve the coin shortage problem. The private minting of coinage came to a close as Congress passed a law in 1864 making it illegal.

Two new denominations of gold coins were introduced in 1849: the twenty-dollar double eagle and the one-dollar coins. Due to the imbalance in the price between gold and silver, the silver dollars were starting to disappear from circulation and the gold dollar was needed to take their place.

The postage rate for a first class letter had risen to three cents in 1851, and this hastened the need for a three-cent coin. The value of the silver three-cent coin was purposely put at 86 percent of the face value; this would prevent of the coin from being removed from circulation to be melted for bullion. Just three years later, the Mint would begin minting three-dollar gold coins. The three-dollar coin was envisioned to allow customers a convenient payment method to purchase one hundred three-cent stamps from the Post Office. They were never popular or really necessary because there were already $2.50 and five-dollar coins in circulation. Nevertheless, the Mint produced the three-dollar gold coin in limited quantities up until 1854.

In order to keep silver coins in circulation, in 1853 the Mint reduced the silver content of the dimes, quarters, and half dollars. They were now issuing "subsidiary" coins, meaning their silver content was below their face value. A set of arrows was placed near the date on all silver coins except three-cent pieces, where the arrows were added to the reverse. The dollars were not affected by the change and their weight remained unchanged. Just a few years later, the arrows were removed as the public had become accustomed to the slight weight reduction. Increased production at the mints and the reduced silver content had the result of there being enough small coins in circulation to facilitate normal trade.

CHAPTER 5

Coinage During the Civil War

By 1857, the copper coinage needed a makeover, the large sized half-cent and cent coins were not popular with the public, and the cost of minting the large sized coins was prohibitive for the Mint. The Coinage Act of 1857 abolished the half-cent and reduced the size and composition of the cent coin. Patterns were struck for the new "Flying Eagle" cent in 1856. This new cent was not made of pure copper but of an alloy of copper and nickel, and it was much smaller than the previous large-sized cent coins. The new cent was short-lived and was only issued for circulation in 1857 and 1858. The new cents were created in large quantities, which almost provided an over-abundance for the business community. The law also required that foreign money circulating be removed from circulation. The Indian Head cent was introduced in 1859 to replace the Flying Eagle cent, and in 1864 its composition was changed and the size was reduced to an even smaller size — the same size as modern cents.

The outbreak of the Civil War had the effect of removing coinage from circulation. The tumult and uncertainty of the war caused people to hoard hard money. Just at the point in history where there was enough small coinage for business, there soon became a shortage. Both the North and the South were producing large quantities of paper money and a premium developed for silver and gold coins, which caused the hard money to be removed from circulation.

Just like the 1830s, when there was a shortage of coinage, the merchants, banks, cities, and even some individuals started to produce their own forms of tokens and script to keep the lines of commerce moving. Some people made use of the three-cent postage stamps to make change. In 1863, many small cent-sized tokens were issued as a substitute for the new small sized pennies. Many had patriotic themes and some looked very similar to the newly introduced Indian Head cents. These tokens had a multitude of uses: they functioned as a medium of exchange, often advertised a merchant's products and location, and they were produced at a profit by the merchant.

Early in the Civil War, religious sentiments were strong, and the Secretary of the Treasury, Salmon P. Chase, started receiving appeals from devout persons throughout the country, urging that the United States acknowledge the deity on coinage. Because of the requests, Secretary Chase instructed the Director of the Mint at Philadelphia, James Pollock, to prepare a motto that expressed a belief in God. Legislation was required for a change in the motto and Congress passed the Act of April 22, 1864, which changed the composition of the one-cent coin and authorized the minting of a two-cent coin with the motto, IN GOD WE TRUST, appearing on the coin. In 1865, Congress passed another Act which allowed the motto to be placed on all gold and silver coins. The motto, IN GOD WE TRUST, has appeared on nearly all United States coins since that time. It wouldn't be until 1957 that the motto started appearing on United States paper money. The two-cent coin was at first popular but then lost favor to the competing one-cent and three-cent coins. The series of two-cent coins only lasted for nine years.

Figure – 1865 Two-Cent Coin

To provide for small denomination currency for trade, the Treasury issued currency notes with a three-cent denomination in 1865. American nickel producers seized upon this change and lobbied for a three-cent coin made of nickel and copper. A law was passed and signed by President Abraham Lincoln in 1865. With the introduction of the copper-nickel three-cent coin and the already existing silver three-cent coin, this made two of the same denomination coins in circulation. Neither coin was that popular and the nickel three-cent piece was struck until 1889, and the silver three-cent piece was minted up until 1873.

The move to a copper-nickel alloy for coinage was underway, and a five-cent coin made of the same copper-nickel alloy as the three-cent piece was introduced. Since there was already a silver half-dime in service, this once again made two coins of the same denomination in circulation at the same time. The silver half-dime was discontinued in 1873. From then on, the five-cent coin would become known as the *nickel*.

CHAPTER 6

The Comstock Lode and the Push for Silver

Just before the start of the Civil War, in 1859, it was made public that silver had been discovered under Mount Davidson in the Virginia range of Mountains in present-day Nevada. This was the first major discovery of silver in the United States, and the silver deposit became known as the Comstock Lode. After the announcement of the find, miners flooded the area and cities, such as Virginia City and Gold Hill, became boom towns. The Comstock Lode greatly increased the amount of silver available for coinage and put a heavy demand on the Philadelphia Mint's production capacity. Silver mining interests applied their considerable political pressure and lobbied for a branch Mint to be opened in Carson City, Nevada. The Mint would allow the assay and minting of silver coins locally rather than having to ship the silver over long distances. The distance from Mount Davidson to the San Francisco Mint was about 250 miles southwest, over some rough country. Carson City, on the other hand, was about 25 miles away — a much more practical distance to haul silver for assay and minting. By the middle of the 1890s, the Comstock Lode was starting to play out and the Carson City Mint closed for good in 1893. Nearly all the gold and silver coins produced by the Mint were in low quantities, and coins from the Carson City Mint, which have the distinctive "CC" Mint mark, are highly sought out by collectors today.

Figure – Comstock Lode Miners circa 1880

The Act of February 21, 1853, which reduced the weight of silver coins, had the effect of demonetizing silver and committed the country to gold as a single standard. By the 1870s, the impact of this law had become known to the silver industry and this began a quarter century of debate and new legislation to return the monetary system to a bimetallism.

Over the years, the government, postmasters, and merchants had accumulated millions of minor coins. To remedy this situation, a law was passed in 1871 that put the minor coins on the same footing as the larger denomination coins. This new law allowed the minor coins to be redeemed in lots of twenty dollars or more.

The laws relating to coinage once again changed in 1873. The new law eliminated the silver dollar and introduced the slightly heavier Trade Dollar. The silver dollar coin had very little circulation and the Treasury felt the removal of a coin that seldom circulated wouldn't impact commerce. The purpose of the Trade Dollar was to be used in trade with the Orient and to compete with the Mexican dollar. The Trade Dollar had a unique place in the history of American coinage in that it was demonetized in 1876. This was done to prevent profiteers from buying the dollars at a reduced rate. The coinage law of 1873 has been referred to as the "Crime of '73." The new law in 1873 called for changes to the weights of the silver dime, quarter, and half dollars. The minor coins, such as the two-cent piece, silver three-cent piece, and the half dime were abolished by this law. The minting of additional minor coins became restricted to the Philadelphia Mint.

The abundant supply of gold was responsible for the decline in the price of gold, which helped precipitate a general business depression in the United States, which hit the Southern and Midwestern states the hardest. The silver interests in the West proposed a return to a bimetallic standard for coinage as a solution to the falling price of gold.

Like the Trade Dollar, a series of coin that had a short life was the silver twenty-cent piece issued in 1875 and 1876. The coin had a specific purpose to allow for change in the Western states. The Spanish "bit" had become equivalent to the dime. Since the five-cent coin did not circulate there, when a quarter was offered for a "bit" purchase, only a dime could be returned in change. The so-called "double dime" looked very similar to the quarter and they were often confused with each other. The twenty-cent piece turned out to be an odd curiosity of history.

CHAPTER 7

The Morgan and Peace Silver Dollars

The five year depression following the financial panic of 1873 caused cheap money advocates, led by Representative Richard Bland of Missouri and Senator William Allison of Iowa, to join with silver producing interests to work toward a bimetallic money system, consisting both of silver and gold. The Bland-Allison Act passed by Congress on February 28, 1878, required minting of the silver dollars once again. The Treasury was to purchase, at market price, two to four million dollars' worth of silver each month to coin into silver dollars. Proponents for the coining of silver contended that with more money in circulation, this would drive workers' wages higher. The opposing business leaders argued against the silver lobby as they believed that the resulting inflation would cheapen the value of money. The Bland-Allison Act was sometimes called "a wretched compromise."

In 1878, production began of a new silver dollar design featuring a left facing bust of Lady Liberty surrounded by the date, legends, and stars. The reverse of the coin has an eagle with outstretched wings, a wreath, legends, and a Mint mark. Today, collectors refer to the type of dollar as the Morgan Dollar, after the English born designer, George T. Morgan. The new silver dollars weren't very popular and hardly circulated in the North and East and ended up back in the Treasury, mainly through tax payments. The Secretary of the Treasury, Daniel Manning, designated the silver dollars as backing for the Silver Certificate Banknotes.

Figure – 1878-CC Morgan Silver Dollar

In 1890, the Bland-Allison Act was repelled and the Sherman Silver Purchase Act took its place in law. The Sherman Act called for 4,500,000 ounces of silver to be purchased each month, paid for with Treasury Notes which were to be legal tender, redeemable in gold or silver dollars that were minted with the purchased silver. The Sherman Act had been pushed through Congress with the backing of wealthy silver miners and farmers. Due to overproduction of crops, prices for the products had fallen dramatically and the farmers' debts were large. They hoped that the infusion of new money into the economy in the form of silver dollars would cause inflation and allow the farmers to pay off their debts with cheaper dollars. The net effect of the Act was that the Treasury Notes were redeemed and the gold and silver was mainly exported. Once the government realized the Act was a failure, it was quickly repealed. The effect of the Bland-Allison Act and the Sherman Act was to add 570 million silver dollars to the nation's monetary system.

Though the Morgan Dollar was still in production in 1921, a new design was introduced to commemorate the end of the Great War. Sculptor and medalist, Anthony de Francisci, was commissioned to develop the new dollar design to be called the Peace Dollar. The obverse of the coin featured Miss Liberty with flowing hair and wearing a spiked tiara, surrounded with legends and dates. The reverse of the coin has an eagle perched before a rising sun surrounded by legends.

The silver dollar had been discontinued in 1904 once all the silver purchased had been turned into coins. In 1918, the Pittman Act provided more silver for minting of the dollars which began again in 1921 with continued production of the Liberty Head or Morgan Dollar design that had been in use since 1878. Though the introduction of a new dollar coin had been suggested by the public since 1918, it wasn't until December of 1921 that the first Peace Dollar was struck. The entire 1921 production of just over one million Peace Dollars was struck in just four days between December 28 and 31. After this first production run, it was apparent that the design, which was a high-relief design, resulted in a very short die life. The excessive force required to force the silver into the deep design features of the dollar dies was causing the dies to wear quickly. In 1922, the design was changed to a low-relief design, thus extending the life of the dies used to strike the coins. The Peace Dollar was stuck until 1935. Like the Morgan Dollars, they weren't very popular with the public and saw limited actual use in day-to-day transactions.

Figure – 1921 Peace Silver Dollar

CHAPTER 8

Twentieth Century Coinage

The country went back under a gold standard in 1900 when President William McKinley signed the Gold Standard Act. The Act established gold as a foundation for US currency and effectively set the price of gold at $20.67 per troy ounce. Paper currency could now be converted into gold at the fixed exchange rate.

Early in the twentieth century, President Theodore Roosevelt became actively involved in the design of new coinage. He was unhappy with the design of coinage and felt they were unattractive. The designs that particularly annoyed the President were the gold coins, which had not changed in decades. President Roosevelt had become acquainted with a gifted sculptor and medalist name Augustus Saint-Gaudens during the creation of a medal honoring Christopher Columbus at the 400th anniversary of the discovery of America.

The ten-dollar gold eagle design was changed to a Saint-Gaudens design, which replaced the head of Miss Liberty with a design where Miss Liberty has a feather war bonnet and the reverse design has a naturalistic eagle inspired by ancient Egyptian silver coins. The Saint-Gaudens design for the twenty-dollar double eagle has Liberty on the obverse striding toward us in the dawn holding the torch of freedom and the olive branch of peace. The reverse of the coin features an eagle soaring above the sun.

Figure – 1907 August Saint-Gaudens Gold Double Eagle

Up until 1933, the metallic worth of US gold coins was equal to the face value of the coin; that is, a ten-dollar coin or "eagle" contained ten dollars' worth of pure gold at current market prices. To encourage a steady flow of gold to the mints, the government had generally adopted a policy of gratuitous coinage, which means that the government bore the cost of converting the gold to coinage.

To commemorate the 100th anniversary of Abraham Lincoln's birth, in 1909 the one-cent coin design was changed from the Indian Head design to a bust of President Lincoln. The reverse of the coin had legends surrounded by two stalks of wheat and the designer's initials, VDB, for Victor David Brenner, were at the bottom of the coin. The designer's initials being on the coin caused a public outcry; many felt that since the designer was paid for his work then his initials should not be on the coin. The initials were deleted from the coin that same year and weren't placed on the coin again until 1918 in a less conspicuous place on the coin. The same design would remain until 1959 when the design was changed to replace the wheat stalks on the reverse with the Lincoln Memorial. At the bicentennial of Lincoln's birth, the reverse was changed once again to four separate designs showing the progression of Lincoln's life from birth in a log cabin, to his formative years, his professional life, and finally, his presidency. Starting in 2010, the reverse design was changed again to the union shield, which is in use today.

In October, 1929, the stock market began an historic meltdown that would take it down to less than half its previous value within three months. Many historians view the stock market crash as the opening act of a long, slow, tumultuous drama that would play out over the next ten-plus years and pull much of the world into a deflationary spiral. At the peak of the depression, one in four able-bodied Americans workers was unemployed and half the banks had gone under. As a result of this trauma to the economy and people's lives, citizens began to hoard hard assets like gold. This placed a burden on the Treasury to redeem the paper money for gold. To stem the flow of gold out of the treasury, President Franklin Roosevelt issued an Executive Order 6102, on April 5, 1933, which prohibited banks from paying out gold or Gold Certificates without permission. The gold coins were being kept in bank vaults for reserve. The intent of the action was to stabilize the price of gold. It had the effect of removing gold coins from circulation and prevented the public from hoarding gold. Newly minted gold and imported gold could only be sold to the government. The executive order was removed in 1974, which again allowed private citizens to accumulate as much gold as they could afford.

Figure – Protestors at a failed bank during the Great Depression.

By the early 1960s, the price of silver had risen to the point where the dimes, quarters, and half dollars in circulation had more value in terms of their silver content than their face value. In 1963, the Treasury Department was concerned that the nation would run out of silver, so to prevent this from happening, the Department hired the Columbus, Ohio-based research company, Battelle Memorial Institute, to investigate the problem. Silver prices had been rising since 1943, when an ounce of silver was under 50 cents. Rising demand, especially from the photography industry, had pushed the price to 90 cents per ounce in 1956. It wasn't until September 1962 that the price of silver reached the breaking point of $1.29 per ounce — this was the price where a dollar's worth of silver coins contained a dollar's worth of pure silver. If the price of silver was to rise above $1.29, the Mint would be producing every dime, quarter, and half dollar at a loss. The Coinage Act of 1965 changed the composition of the dimes and quarters to eliminate the silver from the coins. The Act also required that the silver content of the half dollars be reduced and by 1971, all the silver was gone from regular issue coinage. The new "clad" coins were made from layers of 75% copper and 25% nickel. This composition is still in effect today. The first clad coins were released to the public on November 1, 1965, but the Mint continued to produce silver coins dated 1964 until 1966.

CHAPTER 9

Modern Coinage

Modern American coinage began with the change from silver coins to clad coins in the 1960s. You will rarely find any of the silver dimes, quarters, and half dollars from before 1965 in your pocket change. Modern coinage is really a mix of old and new. The obverse of the Lincoln cent has seen little change since it original debut in 1909; whereas, the reverse has two major changes in design, leaving us with the current reverse design which features a shield and legend. The one-cent coin started as all copper and in 1982 the composition was changed to a zinc center with a thin copper plating on the outside.

The Jefferson nickel came into existence near the end of the Great Depression in 1938. The coin has seen little change except during World War II when the composition was changed to 35 percent silver to help alleviate the shortage of the metal nickel, which was required to support the war effort. The years 2004 and 2005 saw big changes for the Jefferson nickel, with a series of reverses commemorating the bicentennial of the Louisiana Purchase and the Lewis and Clark Expedition.

After the death of President Franklin D. Roosevelt in 1945, the Treasury Department set about the development of a coin to honor the president who had led the nation through the depths of the Great Depression and the hard fought battles of World War II. The ten-cent coin was the logical choice given the president's active support of the March of Dimes' fundraising efforts to cure polio. The Roosevelt dime began production in 1946 with a design that featured a bust of Roosevelt on the obverse and a reverse of a torch flanked by branches of olives and oak.

In 1999, the Mint launched the 50 State Quarters Program which produced a series of 50 quarter-dollar coins with special designs honoring each state. Each year, the United States Mint would release five new quarters in the same order that the states ratified the Constitution. Each quarter's reverse commemorated one of the 50 states with a design emblematic of its unique history, traditions, and symbols. Most of the states let their people have direct input into the reverse deign of their state's quarter. The results of the state's contests were sent to the Secretary of the Treasury for final approval. The State Quarters Program was the most popular commemorative coin program in United States history, with an estimated 147 million Americans collecting state quarters and over three million participating in the selection of state quarter designs.

Figure – Modern Pocket Change

With the average life of a paper one-dollar note being only 18 months, the Mint has always been looking to issue a coin that would circulate in place of the paper dollar note to reduce costs. A coin will typically circulate for twenty years before it has too much wear or damage to be useful. If the Mint could issue a successful dollar coin to replace the short-lived paper dollar notes, then this would be a big cost savings to the Department of the Treasury.

In 1971, the Mint began production of the Eisenhower Dollar, which was a large-sized coin the same size as the Morgan and Peace Dollars. The coin was made of copper-nickel and wasn't a success with the public. This short-lived series lasted only until 1978. The year after the demise of the Eisenhower dollar, the Mint introduced the Susan B. Anthony dollar. The coin was much smaller than the Eisenhower dollar but slightly larger than a quarter. The public confused the coins with the quarter and it didn't see much circulation. Starting in 2008, the Sacagawea dollar coin started circulation. The coin was the same size as the Susan B. Anthony dollar and had a distinctive gold color. The switch to the gold color was to help the public distinguish the coin from a quarter. The obverse of the coin featured the native American Sacagawea, who helped guide the Lewis and Clark Expedition. In 2009, the Sacagawea dollar reverse was changed each year from the soaring eagle to a series of designs that featured Native American scenes.

To honor the past presidents of the United States, a series of one-dollar coins was introduced in 2007. Each year until 2016, four presidents, starting with George Washington, would be honored with their portraits on the obverse of the coins. The coin's reverse has the Statue of Liberty and they are the same size and composition as the Sacagawea dollar. The coins have been popular with collectors but not with the public. In 2011, the Mint gave up on trying to get the coins to circulate and now only strikes the coins for collectors.

CHAPTER 10

Gold and Silver Bullion Program

In 1986, the United States Mint launched a gold and silver bullion coin program. When the program first started, it was primarily a way for the Treasury Department to sell off its excess silver held in the National Strategic Stockpile. With the end of the silver coinage back in the 1960s, the government had a substantial accumulation of silver that they wanted to liquidate without depressing the price of silver. The silver was disposed of in the form of the American Silver Eagle coin. The coin contains one troy ounce of 999 fine silver. The American Silver Eagle one troy ounce bullion coin has been extremely popular with silver collectors and investors. By the early 2000s, the government's silver supply was running low and Congress passed legislation in 2002 allowing the purchase of silver on the open market.

Figure – Modern American Gold and Silver Bullion

At the same time as the Silver Eagles were released, the Mint came out with four gold bullion coins ranging from a tenth-ounce, five-dollar denomination coin to a full one-ounce, fifty-dollar denomination coin. The gold bullion coins are 0.917 fine gold and the designs are a modified Saint-Gaudens striding Liberty on the obverse and a family of eagles on the reverse. The original legislation for the American Eagle gold coins specified that the gold must come from newly mined US gold when it was available.

A decade after the kick-off of the gold and silver bullion programs, the Mint introduced a series of platinum bullion coins. They began in 1997 and, like the gold series, they consisted of tenth-ounce, quarter-ounce, half-ounce, and one-ounce platinum coins. The series lasted until 2008 and all the mintage figures for the series are low. A one-ounce commemorative platinum coin is still produced each year.

Glossary

alloy - To alloy a precious metal is to introduce a quantity of another metal into it. Gold may be alloyed with base metal or with silver. As an example, White Gold is an alloy of gold and nickel or palladium.

assay - The official determination, by a licensed assayer, of the bullion content in an object (usually a gold or silver bar). The assaying of metal requires testing that includes a measurement of its weight by specific gravity.

bullion – A precious metal, such as gold or silver that is in the form of bars, rounds, plates, or coins, that trades strictly based on the intrinsic value of the precious metal content.

commemorative coin – A coin designed to commemorate a particular person or historical event. An example is the first United States commemorative coin, which was an 1892 half-dollar with the image of Christopher Columbus on the obverse and the flagship *Santa Maria* on the reverse.

Figure – 1893 Columbus Commemorative Half Dollar

designer – The artist responsible for a coin's design features.

die – A piece of hardened metal used in the minting of one side of a coin. A pair of dies are required to make the obverse and reverse of a coin during the minting process.

double eagle – A United States twenty-dollar gold coin.

eagle – A United States ten-dollar gold coin. Can also refer to United States silver, gold, and platinum bullion coins made from 1986 to the present.

engraver – The person who sculpts a model for use in translating to a coin die.

fineness – The purity of a precious metal. For example, a United States silver dime is 900 fine, or it is 90% pure silver.

hub – A positive-image punch used in the minting process to impress the coin's design into a die.

legend – A principle inscription on a coin; for example, "United States of America."

obverse – The front side of a coin.

pattern coin – An experimental coin that is used to test a new design or metal composition.

planchet – A piece of metal, typically round, on which a coin design will be stamped.

reverse – The back side of a coin.

token – A money substitute, not issued by a government, that typically has an exchange value in goods or services.

troy ounce – Weights 31.1 grams and is a unit of measure for precious metals.

Acknowledgments

I would like to thank Lisa Zahn for help in preparation of this book.

Further Reading

Bowers, Q. David. *Silver Dollars & Trade Dollars of the United States, A Complete Encyclopedia*, Volume two, Published by Bowers and Merena Galleries, Inc. 1993.

Conant, Charles A. and Doug West. *Alexander Hamilton – Illustrated and Annotated*. C & D Publications. 2015.

Mercanti, John M. *American Silver Eagles – A Guide to the U.S. Bullion Coin Program*. Whitman Publishing LLC. 2013.

Yeoman, R.S. and K. Bressett (editor), *A Guide Book of United States Coins*, Deluxe Edition, Whitman Publishing LCC, 2015.

About the Author

Doug West is a retired engineer, small business owner, and an experienced non-fiction writer with several books to his credit. His writing interests are general, with expertise in science, history, biographies, numismatics, and "How to" topics. Doug has a B.S. in Physics from the Missouri School of Science and Technology and a Ph.D. in General Engineering from Oklahoma State University. He lives with his wife and little dog, "Scrappy," near Kansas City, Missouri. Additional books by Doug West can be found at http://www.amazon.com/Doug-West/e/B00961PJ8M. Follow the author on Facebook at: https://www.facebook.com/30minutebooks.

Figure – The Author Doug West

Additional Books in the "30 Minute Book Series"

A Short Biography of the Scientist Sir Isaac Newton

A Short Biography of the Astronomer Edwin Hubble

Galileo Galilei – A Short Biography

Benjamin Franklin – A Short Biography

The American Revolutionary War – A Short History

The Astronomer Cecilia Payne-Gaposchkin – A Short Biography

Dr. Walter Reed – A Short Biography

Index

Made in the USA
Monee, IL
01 April 2022

93970893R00036